LET THE GAMES BEGIN

written by Rosalie Mastaler & Hunter Mastaler

illustrated by
Betty Yuku

CFI · An Imprint of Cedar Fort, Inc. · Springville, Utah

To all the brave athletes who have paved the path and changed the world of sports. Because of you, sports are now for everybody and every BODY.
You have and will continue to move mountains.

—R. M. and H. M.

ISBN 13: 978-1-4621-4762-5
ebook ISBN 13: 978-1-4621-4831-8

Published by CFI, an imprint of Cedar Fort, Inc.
2373 W. 700 S., Suite 100, Springville, UT 84663
Distributed by Cedar Fort, Inc., www.cedarfort.com

Cover design by Betty Yuku and Shawnda T. Craig

Printed in the United States of America

10 9 8 7 6 5 4 3 2 1

Printed on acid-free paper

Did you know that sports do not end where disability begins?

Check out some of the sports created so everyone can be an athlete. Watch them swim, run, dribble, ski, hit baseballs, and more.

Sports are for every BODY!

Skiers lean left, right, left—*shhhk, swoosh, shhhk.* The ski carves the slope. White powder sprays.

They zoom down the mountain to the finish line.

ALPINE SKIERS have either a visual impairment or a physical disability. Those with a visual impairment use sighted guides and sometimes a headset or a speaker on their back. If one has a lower limb difference, they can sit or stand on one or two skis.

Wheelchairs collide. *CRASH! SMASH!*
Players battle for possession of the ball.

They dodge and juke down the court,
pushing all the way to the goal line.

WHEELCHAIR RUGBY is the combination of three sports—rugby, wheelchair basketball, and hockey. Their chairs can cost up to $10,000! It is one of the only full contact sports in the Summer Paralympic Games making it ONE OF A KIND! Wheelchair rugby made its first appearance at the 1996 Paralympic Games.

Shhhh, quiet. Listen for the beeping baseball.
The blindfolded batter steps up to the plate.

The pitcher winds up and . . . *CRACK!*
The ball flies through the air.
Run, run, run, to the buzzing base!

BEEP BASEBALL is played with only two bases. Each base buzzes so the players can hear where they need to run. There are six innings as opposed to the traditional nine. Also, 1, 2, 3, and . . . *4* strikes, you're out.

Swimmers pull on their caps.
They position their goggles
and get set on the block.

"Swimmers ready." *BZZZ! SPLASH!*

SWIMMING is one of the original sports of the first Paralympic Games in 1960, with only 77 original participants. The sport has grown to be one of the largest and most popular of the Paralympics. 606 swimmers competed at the 2020 Tokyo Games.

**They dive in and pull through each stroke.
They kick and reach for the wall.**

Wheels roll. Players dribble.
Up and down the court they pass, block, and shoot.

SWOOSH, goes the ball into the net.
SCORE!

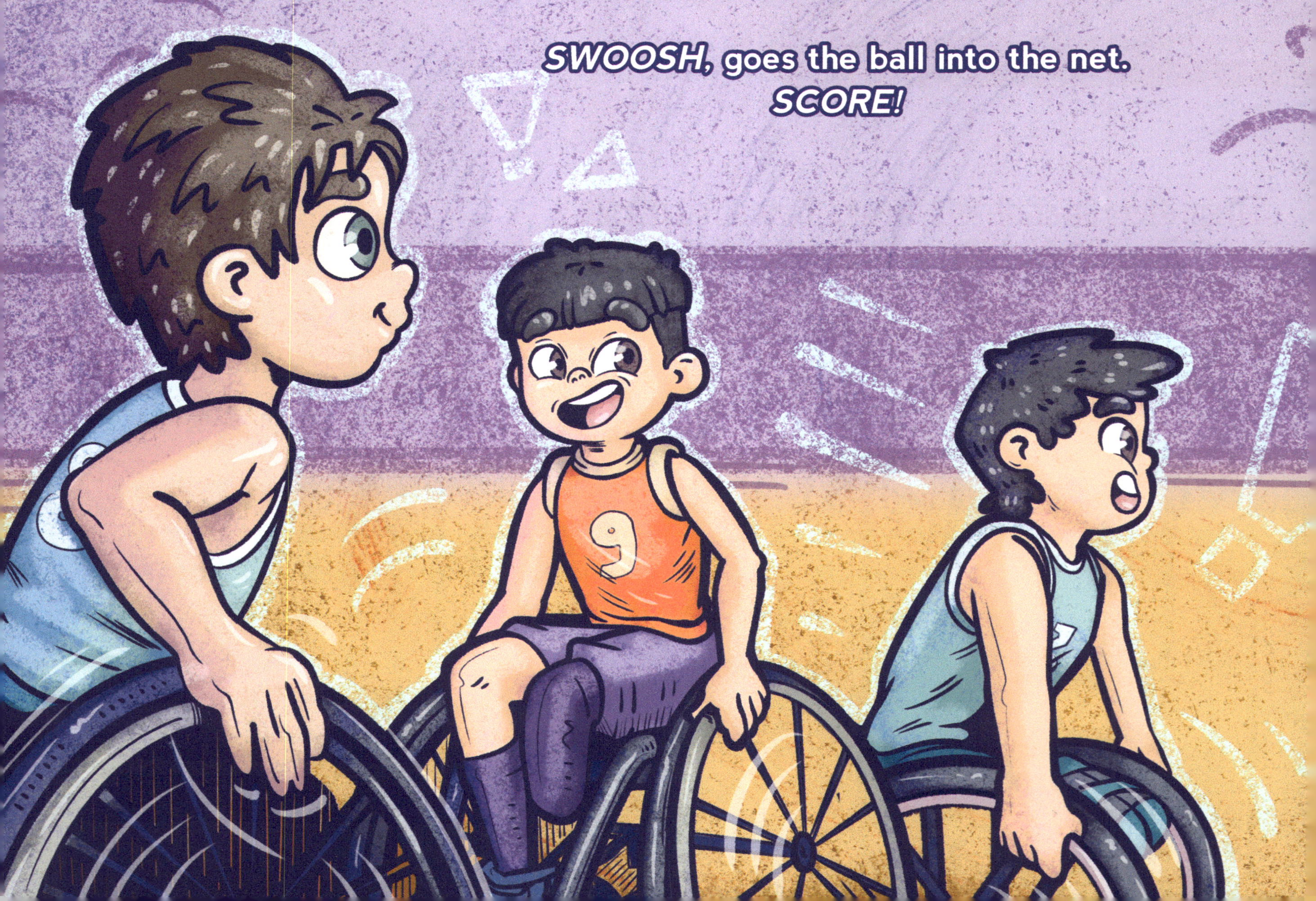

WHEELCHAIR BASKETBALL was developed as a direct result of World War II because of the mass injuries that occurred. Many athletes wanted to be involved in sports but needed them to be adapted to their abilities. Wheelchair basketball was one of the first sports on the adaptive sporting scene. It has been loved and revered ever since its development. Today, hundreds of thousands of people play the sport in over 100 countries worldwide.

"QUIET PLEASE."

The referee silences the audience.

A ball flies through the air.

RING A-LING A-LING!

Bells ring inside the ball.

Blindfolded players lunge toward the sound to defend their goal.

GOALBALL is where players wear blindfolds to create an even playing field with blind participants. The referees silence the crowd before the ball goes into play, making it a quiet game. With only three players per team on the court at a time, a ball with bells inside is thrown underhand toward the opponents net in hopes of scoring a goal.

SLED HOCKEY is played with two shortened hockey sticks with a blade on one end and a metal pick on the other enabling players to hit the puck or propel themselves across the ice. USA is the team to beat! They've won 5 gold medals, the most in Paralympic history for sled hockey, in 2002, 2010, 2014, 2018, and 2022.

Sled hockey players glide across the ice—*sfft, sfft.*

The puck is hit and passed.
He shoots for the net!
BUZZZZZ!
A goal is scored
at the last second!

SITTING VOLLEYBALL is played on a court that is smaller than a traditional volleyball court. The net is closer to the ground and stands at 45 inches tall for men and 39 inches tall for women. It is against the rules for players to lift their torso or bottom off the ground.

Players slide and scoot
around the court.
Serve, rally, set, spike,
block, attack and . . .

"OUT!" yells the referee.
The ball is out of bounds.

Archers take their position.
Arrows are drawn.

She aims at the target.
WOOSH! BULLSEYE!
A perfect shot, straight down the middle.

ARCHERY is another original sport of the Paralympics and like its counterpart at the Olympic Games, uses the same equipment, rules, and format. Archers receive 10 points if they hit a bullseye—an arrow directly in the middle of the target. Archers can draw the bow with their teeth, compete from a sitting position, or use aids like a tripod for those with a visual impairment.

The starter pistol fires. *BANG!*
Prosthetic running blades pound the track.

RUNNERS with a lower limb difference use prosthetic running blades made out of carbon fiber. Depending on the size of the runner, approximately thirty to ninety sheets of carbon fiber are fused together to create a lightweight and almost indestructible running blade. However, some runners have been known to break a blade while running.

Racers pump their arms.
They bolt toward the finish line.

Slipping and sliding down the glistening ice, the stone glides toward the target.

WHEELCHAIR CURLING originates from a sport that was invented during medieval times. It was adapted for wheelchair users in the 1990's making its Paralympic debut in 1998. The curling stones are made from a rare granite from a remote island off the coast of Scotland.

CLACK! Stones collide.
One stays, the other one goes out. *SUCCESS!*

Wheels spin and roll.
Players rush the ball.

She swings her racket and . . .
SMASH! The ball flies over the net.

Her opponent misses. *SCORE!*

WHEELCHAIR TENNIS uses the same scoring system as tennis. One major difference is that wheelchair tennis players can let the ball bounce twice before they hit it. In 1992 there were only 11 international tournaments. Today, there are more than 160 tournaments in over 40 countries, and the popularity of the sport continues to grow.

The long jumper pulls down his blindfold and listens for his guide.

"FLY! FLY! FLY!"

He runs at super speed.

BLIND LONG JUMPERS wear blindfolds, just like goalball, so everyone has an equal chance. They don't use guide runners. Instead, they use verbal guides who stand at the end of the runway. The longest blind long jump is 22 feet by world record holder, Lex Gillette.

He jumps.
He flies.
He lands in the sand.

He sets a ***WORLD RECORD!***
The crowd goes wild!

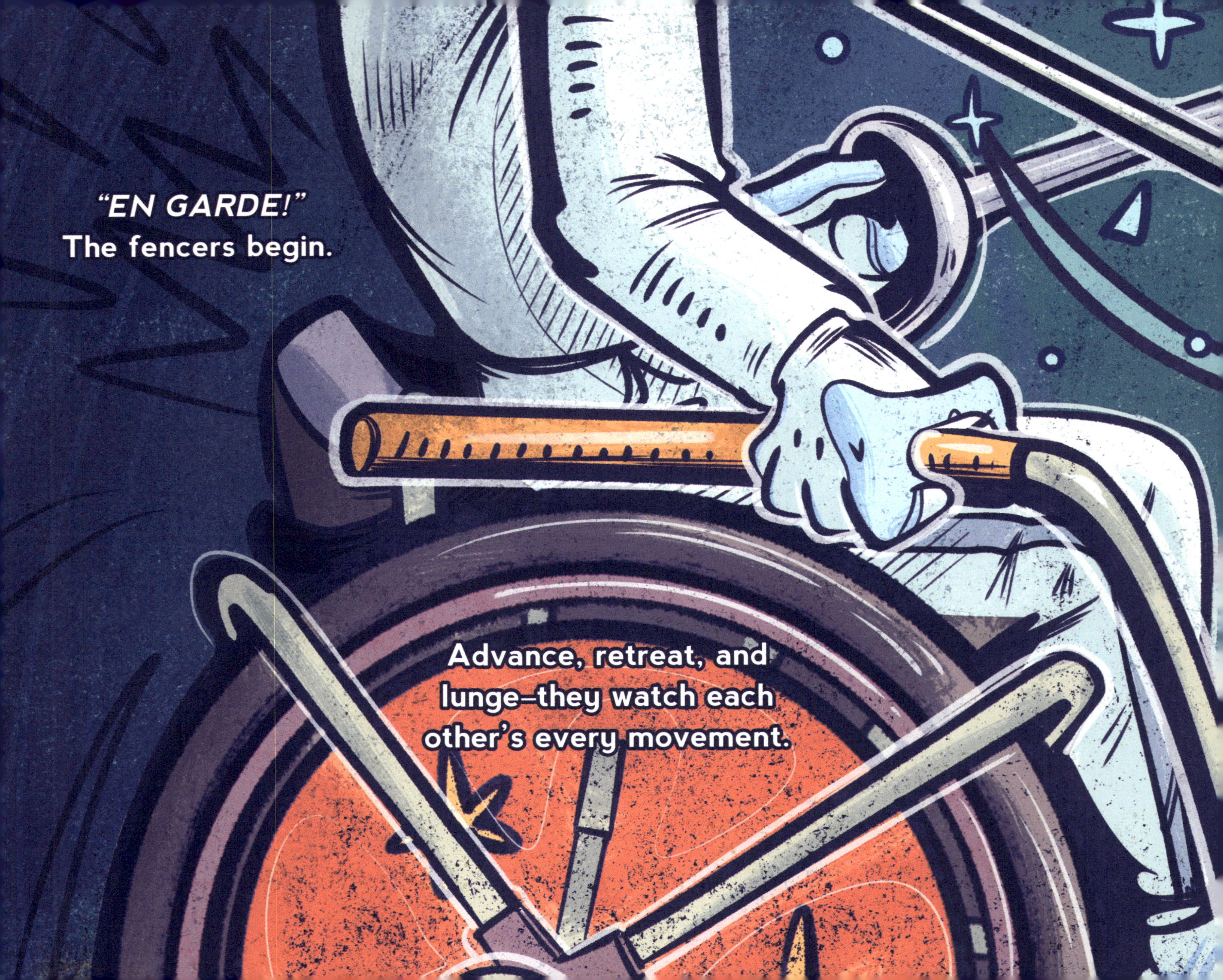

"EN GARDE!"
The fencers begin.

Advance, retreat, and lunge–they watch each other's every movement.

They dodge and dart to avoid the sword.

WHEELCHAIR FENCING is another original sport that debuted in the 1960 Paralympics. A wheelchair fencer's wheelchair is secured to the ground and all the movement comes from the athlete. One scores in wheelchair fencing by touching the end of the blade to their opponent's upper body.

YAY! YOU CAN DO IT!
The audience claps. Eyes are wide. Cheers are loud.

CLINK. CLANK. A medal hangs around the athlete's neck.
From the podium, they smile and wave. *I DID IT!*
Sports are for every BODY.